What Was It Like Growing Up in the 90s?

A Journal to Revisit and Share the Rad 90s

~ Riya Aarini ~

This book
belongs to '90s kid

_____

_____

Contents

Welcome to Your '90s History!

The 1990s was an idyllic time to grow up. Kids played outside for hours, returning home once it got dark or their parents called. For the last generation without cell phones, life was refreshingly simpler.

The internet was in its infancy and, though fun, hadn't developed into an all-consuming distraction. Grappling with less information from the world wide web, children spent their days carefree. Social interactions radiated a genuineness, as kids visited friends rather than "talked" over text. A welcome sense of wholesomeness infused the decade.

Around the corner, the new millennium stirred excitement about the possibilities for the future. Technology improved steadily—without being excessive—and offered everyone hope.

Via this journal, return to a less-complicated era from which some of the best movies, fashion, and music emerged. The '90s was a magical, optimistic decade that remains second to none!

Birthdays

List five radical birthday gifts you received in the '90s.

_____

_____

_____

_____

_____

Common '90s bithday party venues included the arcade, skating rink, bowling alley, pizzeria, at home.

Where did you celebrate your birthdays?

Did you throw slumber parties for your birthdays? If so, describe an unforgettable one.

Did you bring cupcakes for the entire class on your birthday?

Were your birthday cakes topped with trick candles?

Did you enjoy homemade birthday cakes or cakes from the bakery? If homemade, who baked them?

Describe a memorable birthday party invitation.

How did your party guests RSVP?

School

What was your favorite class?

How did you learn to type? On an electric typewriter, a word processor?

Did you pass handwritten notes in class?

Describe one of the funniest or most embarrassing.

Describe a time a teacher intercepted and read the note out loud.

How well did you perfect the origami-like folding?

What foods did school lunches consist of?

How much did a small carton of milk or chocolate milk cost?

Were you ever sent to detention? If so, why?

Did you write book reports to earn coupons to the local pizzeria for a free personal pan pizza? If so, how did it feel to redeem the vouchers?

Did your teacher announce that your school was among the last to be taught cursive, due to the introduction of computers?

If you learned cursive in school, do you feel privileged to be a part of one of the last generations to read and write cursive?

Yearbooks

Did you sign your classmates' elementary, junior high, or high school yearbooks?

Do you recall any memorable messages, inside jokes, or well-wishes?

How important was it to you to autograph yearbooks or have yours autographed?

Extracurricular Activities

What extracurricular activities did you participate in?

If you were in the school band, what instrument did you play?

If you were athletic, what sports did you play?

If you served on the school newspaper, what was your role?

Graduation

How did it feel to graduate elementary school, middle school, or high school in the '90s?

Describe your graduation ceremony, if your school had one.

What are your best memories of graduation?

Friends

The limited technology (social media, emails, texts) in the '90s meant the basis of friendships rested on genuine face-to-face interactions, loyalty, and play.

Did you have a few or many friends growing up in the '90s?

How did you bond with your childhood friends? Movies, music, hobbies?

Did you talk on a corded or cordless landline with friends?

How long did your phone conversations last?

Did you host or attend sleepovers? What were they like?

Was camp a part of your childhood? Describe the best and worst of camp.

Did you knock on friends' doors to ask if they could come out and play?

Friendship Bracelets

Did you weave friendship bracelets with colorful thread?

Did you trade friendship bracelets at camp, school, elsewhere?

How many friendship bracelets did you wear at a time on your wrists?

Did you ever take the friendship bracelets off? If not, how tattered did they get?

Were friendship bracelets a status symbol of your '90s childhood?

Did you feel you had the freedom to be a kid in the '90s?

How would you describe the quality of friendships in the '90s?

Fashion

Fashion in the '90s included baggy jeans and denim: denim overalls, denim jeans, denim dresses, and denim jackets. Streetwear grew in global popularity, ushering in a bold, new era of fashion.

What fashion style did you adopt in the '90s?

Did you dress in the rebellious '90s grunge style? If so, describe your typical go-to outfit.

Sneaker Culture

Sneaker culture soared to impressive heights in the '90s.

Did you wear chunky '90s athletic sneakers?

Did you own a sneaker collection? If so, describe it.

What was your favorite brand of sneakers?

Do you still wear '90s style sneakers?

Do you think today's shoes pale in comparison to cool '90s sneakers?

What '90s fashion trend did you try and like?

What '90s fashion trend did you try and dislike?

Hair

The '90s started to see a deflation of the infamous, big '80s hair.

Did you add highlights to your '90s hairdo?

The bodacious '80s curls stepped aside for the sleek '90s hair. How did you style your hair in the '90s?

Holidays

Valentine's Day

How did you celebrate the day of love in the '90s?

Did you pass out cardstock Valentine's Day cards to classmates?

Did you receive Valentine's Day cards from classmates? If so, do you still have them, like tucked away in a box in the attic?

Did you decorate a Valentine's Day box for class the night before to collect cards and candy?

Did you munch on Valentine's Day treats? If so, which ones?

July the Fourth

How did you celebrate Independence Day in the '90s?

Did you light sparklers or go big with fireworks?

Did you watch or join the Fourth of July parades? Describe the feelings they inspired.

Halloween

List three dope Halloween costumes you wore in the '90s.

_____

_____

_____

Did you wear plastic or handmade costumes? If homemade, who sewed them?

Did you trick-or-treat? What did you use to collect candy: plastic bucket, paper bag, pillow case?

What did you think about homes that gave out king-size candy bars?

What was your favorite Halloween candy? What was your least favorite?

Did you trade candy with fellow trick-or-treaters?

Did your parents impose a tax on your Halloween candy?

List one unusual thing you received while trick-or-treating.

How late did you stay out freely roaming the streets on Halloween night?

Did you play Ouija boards and Bloody Mary?

Did you watch Halloween specials on TV? If so, which ones?

Did you play Halloween pranks on unsuspecting adults? If so, describe one!

How magical was Halloween in the '90s?

Politics

US Presidents

Did you watch Bill Clinton's 1993 Presidential Inauguration?
If so, on TV or in person?

If you attended or watched, describe the atmosphere.

What did you think about President Bill Clinton's 1998 impeachment for the scandal involving a White House intern?

Cold War

How did you react to the collapse of the Soviet Union in 1991?

How did you feel about the end of the Cold War?

Books

Name five books you enjoyed in the '90s.

_____

_____

_____

_____

_____

List your most-read book series.

Did you perform extra chores to earn money to buy books?

How often did you visit the library to check out books?

Popular '90s authors included Shel Silverstein, Judy Blume, and Roald Dahl.

Who were your favorite authors?

Did you think the books, such as Michael Crichton's "Jurassic Park," were better than the movies? If so, how?

News

Newspapers

Did your family buy newspapers from the newsstand or subscribe to home deliveries?

Magazines

What '90s magazines did you subscribe to or buy individually?

Movies

Popular '90s movies included
1990: "Home Alone"
1993: "Jurassic Park"
1995: "Jumanji"

Name three sweet '90s movies.

_____

_____

_____

Did you go to the local theater to watch movies?

Did you rent VHS tapes to watch movies at home on a VCR?

Did you rent an extra movie, since the first was a gamble?

How long did it take to pick out a movie to rent?

Did you rewind the VHS tapes before returning them to the video store? How did you feel about this policy?

How many VHS tapes did you have in your home?

Do you feel '90s movies had a sense of fun, charm, originality, and humor—making them highly entertaining and enjoyable?

Do you consider the '90s to be the greatest decade for movies? Why or why not?

Television

Did you tape TV shows on a VCR?

Did you rush home after school to watch TV? If so, which shows?

What were your favorite television sitcoms or dramas?

Did you refer to the "TV Guide" to catch shows?

How many channels did your '90s television have?

Do you feel television was exceptional in the '90s? Why or why not?

Internet

What was the first computer you used in the '90s?

What did you use it for? Games, typing?

When was the first time you used the internet?

Did you have dial-up internet? How did you feel when you had to disconnect so a family member could use the phone?

Did your family get a separate phone line for internet usage?

Did you join online chat rooms?

How slow was the internet dial-up speed?

How long did it take to load a page? Did you engage in other activities while you waited?

How did it feel to have the internet's vast knowledge at your fingertips?

Do you recall the sound of dial-up internet? If so, do you find it nostalgic?

Conversations

Did you pepper your speech with popular '90s slang?

Do you catch yourself still using these words today?

Did you enjoy the face-to-face conversations of the '90s?

Did you feel more connected to people (the music store clerk, strangers on the bus, or even friends) in the '90s?

Flashes from the '90s Past

Flashes from the '90s Past

Music

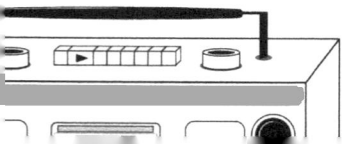

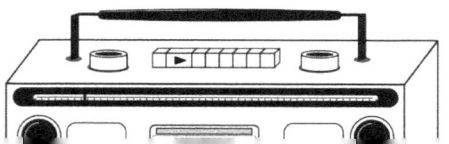

What were your favorite '90s music genres?

Which music artists or bands did you enjoy most?

List three songs you couldn't resist playing on repeat.

_____

_____

_____

If you listened to the radio, how did it feel when your favorite song played by chance?

Music Videos

Did you watch MTV or VH1?

List your three favorite music videos.

_____

_____

_____

Did you record music videos on VHS?

CDs

Did you visit the CD stores?

Name three CDs you bought in the '90s.

_____

_____

_____

Did you own a portable CD player? Where did you listen to it?

Mixtapes

Did you create your own mixtapes?

Did you make mixtapes for friends?

Did you create and give mixtapes to romantic interests? If so, how did they respond?

Considering the time and effort it took to create mixtapes, what significance did they hold for you?

Staying Connected

Answering Machines

Did your family use an answering machine?

What was one of the funniest answering machine messages you'd heard?

Cordless Phones

Did you dial friends and family using a cordless phone?

Did you memorize friends' phone numbers?

Cell Phones

Did you own a cell phone?

If so, where did you carry it?

Pay Phones

Did you carry around quarters in case you needed to use a pay phone?

How much did you rely on pay phones in the '90s?

Did you ever call collect? Give an example of a time you asked the operator to make a collect call.

Did you ever find coins in the coin return? How thrilled did you feel?

Phone Books

How often did you use the phone book? Whose numbers did you look up?

Did your family pay the phone book company to keep your number unlisted?

Did you comb through the phone book, looking for people with the same name as you?

Did you ever prank call someone using a number listed in the phone book? Describe the prank!

Letters

Did you write letters with a pen or pencil on decorative stationery?

Did you receive any letters that became your favorites?

Do you still have these letters, like in a keepsake box?

Greeting Cards

What were some of the most memorable greeting cards you received in the '90s?

Did you print homemade greeting cards, fold them into quarters, and give them away?

Prom

Did you go to prom? If so, what did you wear? What did your date wear?

Did you go all out on prom night with a limo and fancy dinner? If not, what fun prom activities did you enjoy?

Did you take the traditional prom photo? Would you describe it as cringeworthy or memorable? What made it so?

What was your prom song?

Was it performed by a live band?

What lasting memories did prom celebrations create?

Dating

Where did you take your date? Or where did your date take you?

Did your date ask your parents for permission before taking you out?

Did you receive mixtapes with romantic songs? What did they tell you about the giver?

Were you ever late to a date and missed it entirely (because you didn't yet have the convenience of texting that you were running behind)?

Did you feel dating was simpler in the '90s? Why or why not?

Do you feel dating was more authentic in the '90s, considering it required face-to-face interactions?

Video Games

Did you play video games in the '90s? If so, on a home console or at the arcades? If at the arcades, describe the experience.

What were your favorite video games?

Do you feel video games advanced in the '90s? How so?

Do you consider the '90s to be the golden era of video games?
Why or why not?

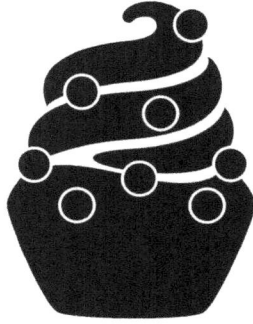

Food

Did your family dine at all-you-can-eat buffets? For some families, this was a highly anticipated ritual.

What was your favorite buffet restaurant?

What menu items did you enjoy most?

As a kid, did you eat free at the buffets? How cool was that?

What was your favorite homecooked meal?

What were your favorite '90s snacks?

Celebrities

Who were your favorite '90s celebrities in music, movies, or sports?

What did you admire about them?

Did you get to meet any of them in person? If so, where?

Leisure Activities

'90s kids stayed active, riding their bikes around the neighborhood, jumping in the pool, or exploring the woods.

What physical activities did you participate in during the '90s?

Summer

Summer Vacations

Summer was a time for water balloon fights, BBQs, ice cream, popsicles, watching cartoons on Saturday mornings, and climbing trees.

What did you do during the never-ending summer vacations?

Family Vacations

Did your family vacation when school was out for the summer?

Describe one memorable family vacation spot.

Did your family consult large paper maps during road trips?

If you took family road trips, what car games did you play?

Did the family car have A/C?

What memories did family road trips create?

Bedroom

What posters hung on your '90s bedroom wall?

Did a lava lamp light up your bedroom with vibrant neon colors? What inspired you to add it to your bedroom?

Did glow-in-the-dark stars shine on your bedroom ceiling?

Hobbies

What hobbies did you enjoy in the '90s?

Did you have any prize collections, like baseball cards, stamps, or coins?

Malls

Was mall culture a big part of your '90s youth?

How often did you hang out at the mall with friends?

What did you find appealing about walking around the sea of stores, kiosks, arcades, movie theaters, and eateries?

Jobs

Common jobs for '90s kids included babysitter, fast food, newspaper delivery, and record or video store.

If you worked in the '90s, what jobs did you hold?

How much did you earn?

What did you spend your earnings on?

Lemonade Stands

Did you operate a lemonade stand?

If so, how much did you charge per cup?

Did you turn a profit?

How did you advertise? Posterboard signs, word-of-mouth?

Intangibles

What was your biggest takeaway of the decade?

What goals did you set for yourself in the '90s? Did you achieve them?

Describe one major accomplishment you are most proud of.

Did '90s culture give you any aha moments? If so, what was one of them?

What about the '90s are you most grateful for?

In the '90s, who did you want to be, professionally or personally, when you grew up?

Who was your '90s hero, real or imagined? Why did you look up to them?

How did you experience life before the encroachment of technology (social media, email, texts)?

Growing up in the '90s, what did you most want to change about the world?

What was an average day like in the '90s?

Describe your best, most unforgettable day.

Describe your worst, most forgettable day.

What aspects of the '90s excited you?

What values did you hold in the '90s?

What was the biggest risk you took in the '90s?

What would have made the '90s better than it was?

What about the '90s do you wish continued to the present day?

What was it like to celebrate New Year's Eve in 1999?

Sum up the '90s in one word.

_____

More Flashes from the '90s Past

More Flashes
from the '90s Past

Long Live the '90s!

Answering these prompts might've returned you to carefree times, even if for a splendid moment. By sharing the completed journal, your loved ones gain insights into a slice of the special '90s culture that you are privileged to have been an important part of. Now that's rad!

Books in the
What Was It Like series

What Was It Like Growing Up in the 70s?
A Journal to Revisit and Share the Groovy 70s

What Was It Like Growing Up in the 80s?
A Journal to Revisit and Share the Totally Awesome 80s

What Was It Like During Christmas in the 80s?
A Journal to Revisit and Share the 80s Holiday Spirit

What Was It Like Fooding in the 80s?
A Journal to Revisit and Share 80s Totally Tubular Eats

What Was It Like During Christmas in the 90s?
A Journal to Revisit and Share the 90s Holiday Vibe

What Was It Like Marrying in the 90s?
A Journal (for Her) to Revisit and Share 90s Wedding
Magic